Department of the Environment
Ancient Monuments and Historic Buildings

D1744742

The Fortifications of Berwick-upon-Tweed

IAIN MACIVOR BA, FSA
Inspector of Ancient Monuments

LONDON: HER MAJESTY'S STATIONERY OFFICE

ISBN 0 11 670428 4

Contents

History

Medieval defences

When Margaret of Norway died in 1290, the succession to the Scottish throne was disputed. Edward I of England arbitrated between the claimants in his alleged right as Lord Superior. In 1292 he declared John Baliol King of Scotland in the hall of Berwick Castle.

The prosperous royal burgh had been part of Scotland for more than three centuries. In 1292 the town itself lacked any significant defences. It occupied the western part of a peninsula formed by the Tweed estuary and the sea. Adjoining the town to the north-west was the castle, overlooking the Tweed.

An appeal made over Baliol's head to Edward in a Berwick lawsuit caused the first friction between the kings. Edward's feudal claims on Baliol soon led to disaffection in Scotland and to a defensive alliance between Scotland and France. English policy was continued by war. Berwick was captured in 1296. A swift punitive campaign through Scotland persuaded Baliol to abdicate and his nobility to submit.

Four days after the capture of Berwick, workmen were ordered to the town to fortify it. A ditch, bank and wooden palisade were rapidly constructed. Magdalen Fields, east of the town and undeveloped up to the present day, was excluded. On the lines established in 1296, the town walls were rebuilt, strengthened and repaired for the next 260 years. The first improvements began in 1297–98 when a start was made to replace the palisade by a stone wall. Building continued throughout Edward's reign.

At the castle, the south-east defences facing the town were strengthened. The side of the castle towards the town, with the main entrance, was low and vulnerable if the town fell into unfriendly hands, so it required special attention. The surviving polygonal south tower of the castle is part of a complete remodelling of the south-east front, though it is not clear whether the remodelling was undertaken in the reign of Edward I or Edward III. Works were carried on elsewhere at the castle, and the spectacular stepped White Wall running from the castle down to the Tweed probably survives from 1297–98.

Scottish resistance to alien rule, begun under William Wallace, prevailed under Robert Bruce, the son of one of the claimants who had appeared before Edward I in Berwick Castle. Bruce, exploiting his military initiative after Bannockburn, captured Berwick in 1318. The Scots climbed the new walls unseen to win the burgh. Soon the castle too surrendered.

In a ten days' siege during the next year, Edward II attempted to retake Berwick. The walls were still so low in places that the defenders could be struck in the face by a spear-thrust from below. The Scots withstood the siege and then set about raising the walls to an adequate height. For, contrary to Bruce's usual practice, the fortifications were not destroyed. He meant to keep Berwick, and did so during his lifetime.

The exertions which preserved Scotland did not secure her frontier town. On 4 April 1333 Edward III opened a siege of Berwick and, defeating a relieving force at nearby Halidon Hill, occupied it on 20 July. Repairs were begun to buildings in the castle damaged by the siege. Although from this time fairly regular sums were spent by the king's officers on maintenance of the castle, it was not kept in good repair and additional moneys were required. The town walls were normally maintained by the mayor and citizens; its now-elaborate defences—which included nineteen towers with timber fighting-platforms—also did not always receive necessary attention, and a constant watch was necessary against surprise. During the night of 6 November 1355 a party of Scots scaled the walls near the Cowgate and took over the town; Edward hastily returned from France and reoccupied it in January 1356. More improvements to the town walls followed.

Natural decay of walls and buildings was continually aided by the Scots, who briefly occupied the castle in 1378 and 1384, burnt the town in 1383 and looted it in 1405—when the castle was being held against Henry IV by followers of the rebellious Earl of Northumberland.

Henry recovered the castle after operations which included the first recorded use of artillery—then crude weapons of limited effectiveness—against Berwick. Increased sums were spent on the works from 1427, but the English hold on Berwick was relinquished voluntarily in 1461, when Queen Margaret surrendered the town and castle to the Scots in return for their support of the Lancastrian cause in the Wars of the Roses.

Berwick was retaken by the English in 1482 after a long siege. The town did not change hands again.

Fortification against cannon

In the middle ages, high walls and flanking towers offered security against surprise and could be successfully defended against direct assault. The damage they might sustain from catapults or other

throwing-engines was limited. Though even the best planned castle
or walled town could be reduced by the combined devices of medieval
siegecraft, it could offer a very protracted resistance.

In the sixteenth century the development of artillery slowly destroyed
the value of traditional fortification. High walls could be demolished
by direct bombardment. To strengthen them they might be lowered
and reinforced. They might also be pierced by gun-ports and provided
with platforms and squat towers to mount defending guns. The first
artillery fortifications are such adaptations of medieval design. It was
an intermediate phase: in western Europe a new kind of fortification

Fifteenth-century guntower on the west wall of the castle

was experimentally worked out to provide effective defence by and against artillery. The development is outstandingly illustrated at Berwick.

In the years immediately after 1482 some new defences were constructed to consolidate the English hold on Berwick. They cannot now be identified; nor can works of 1509–12, reflecting worsening Anglo-Scottish relations before Flodden: they may have been earthworks rather than masonry structures. The earliest clearly identifiable artillery fortifications belong to 1522–23 when a great detached earthwork, the Windmill Bulwark, was raised beyond a shallow salient of the east town wall, and the masonry "Bulwark by the Sands," later called Fisher's Fort, was added to the riverside defences. "Bulwark" was then a loose term to describe artillery strong points of widely different designs: later it was used more specifically for the Italianate angular bastions described below. Other improvements, notably an earthwork at the north-east angle of the town wall, have been obscured.

The north-east angle was vulnerable because, under any method of siege warfare, the town could be attacked from the land on two sides by an enemy infiltrating along Magdalen Fields, with particularly uncomfortable pressure being exerted against the north-east salient. Artillery increased the danger. The earthwork there was replaced in 1539–42 by a circular masonry fortification, later called Lord's Mount. The latter, a massive low-profile work over 100ft in diameter, with 19ft thick walls casemated for artillery, is of outstanding interest as the final development in the transitional stage of artillery fortification, now quite transformed from medieval concepts. Unfortunately the original plans do not survive, as they had an extra dimension of interest. Lord's Mount was not built as proposed because the master-mason responsible for construction disregarded the plans he had been sent; a foolhardy self-confidence, since Henry VIII himself—an able student of fortification—had been concerned with their drawing.

Apparently at the same time as Lord's Mount was being built, much smaller round gun-towers were added to the north-west curtain of the castle and to the riverside end of the White Wall. Other towers in the new style, now lost, may have further reinforced the castle. Near the end of Henry's reign, at the time of Hertford's incursions into Scotland, further improvements in 1544–45 were proposed—in which an Italian engineer was concerned—to add more defensive firepower. In the future it should be possible to recover, by documents and archaeology,

The medieval castle and town walls of Berwick, with major artillery fortifications added by Henry VIII and proposed by Edward VI

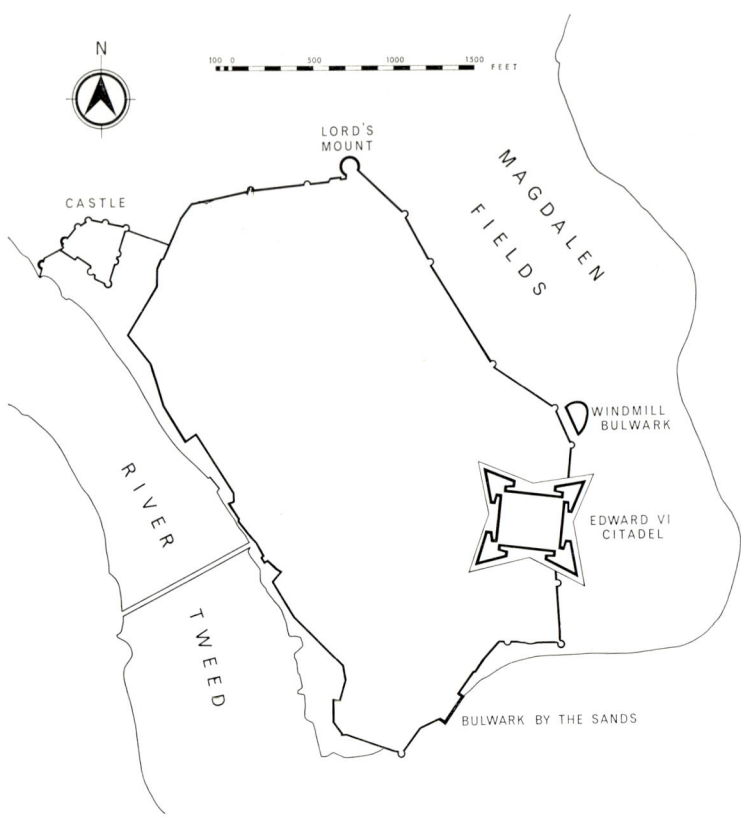

a sharper overall picture of the additions, alterations, renewals and repairs of Henry VIII's reign. The summary and incomplete review above, which does not mention the many rebuilds and patchings of the walls themselves, as distinct from the works attached to them, does, however, indicate a piecemeal transformation of the medieval lines in a costly attempt to keep pace with the changing patterns of siege warfare.

There are hints that some of the lost works of Henry's reign were unarticulated essays in the newest fashion in fortification, then just becoming known in Britain. At first in Italy, a new work called a bastion was developed as a rational design for an artillery fortification.*

---

*Military engineers used special technical terms to describe the parts of a fortification with bastions. These terms are used throughout this handbook; for, although they have the drawback of unfamiliarity, they have the great advantage of precise meaning. A descriptive list of such terms used in the guide, with an explanatory diagram, is given on pages 38–40 at the end of the book.

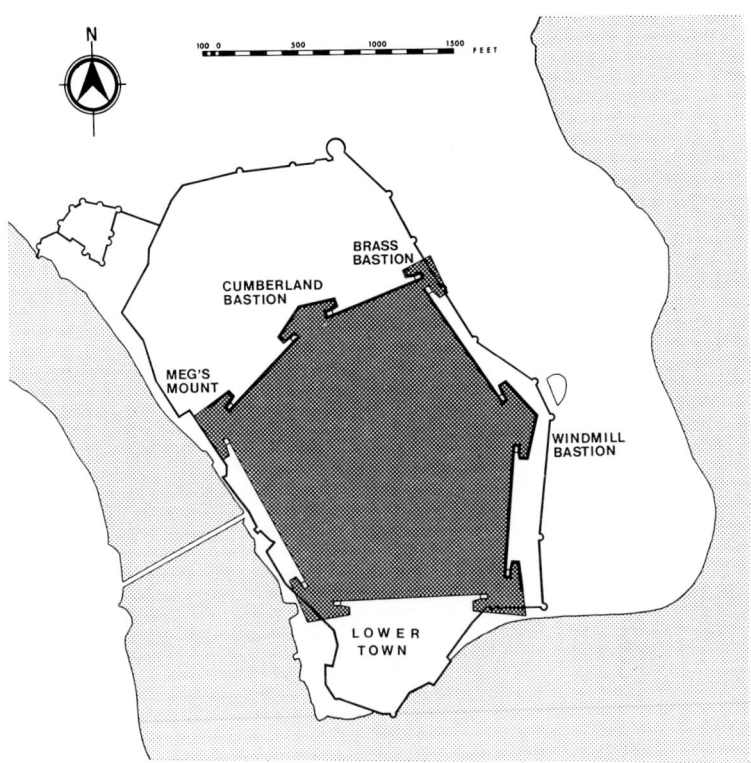

The north and east fronts of the Elizabethan fortifications as built in 1558–61. The intended plan to complete the works is shown with a light line

N

100 0   500   1000   1500 FEET

BRASS BASTION

CUMBERLAND BASTION

MEG'S MOUNT

WINDMILL BASTION

LOWER TOWN

A bastion has two flanks for a concentration of defensive fire-power and two faces for offensive guns firing into the field. The angular plan allowed the flanking guns to open a deadly fire on a close approach to any part of the rampart. The outer walls or scarps of the earth-backed curtains and bastions were low, sloped to increase stability, and protected by a ditch. Systems of bastioned fortification were improved and elaborated for over 250 years.

There is so little left of the earliest systematic bastioned work at Berwick that its remains were not identified until 1960. A square citadel or fort further to strengthen the east side of the town was the major improvement to Berwick proposed in the reign of Edward VI. It was to lie across the medieval wall on commanding high ground. Little is known of it save its outline ground plan. Work on the citadel in 1550–52 costing £16 700 seems to have finished that part of it

The state of the fortifications in 1569, when building was
suspended. The new landward ramparts are usable though
incomplete: the medieval wall is still the defence along
the river side

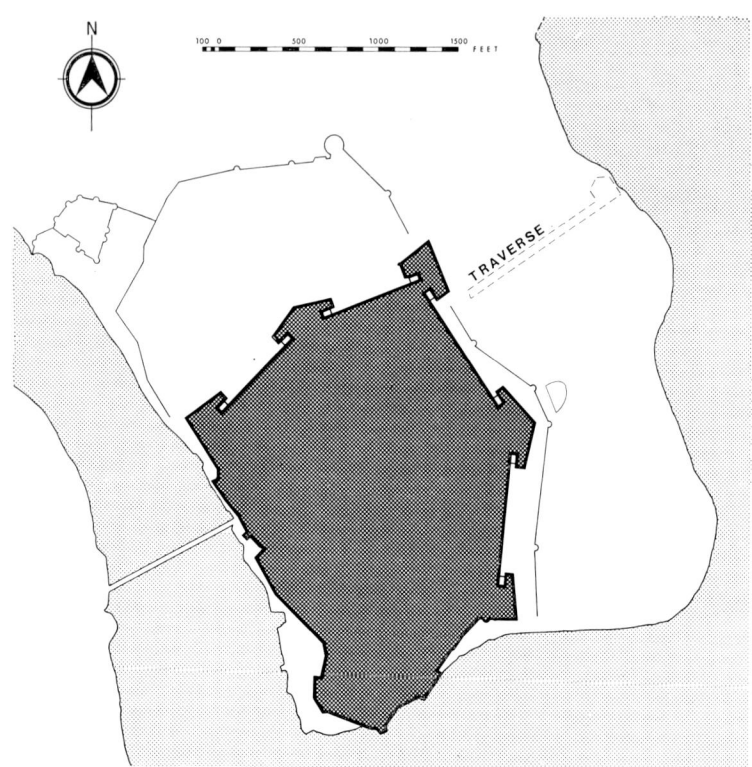

within the medieval town wall. After a five-year delay, work was
started in Mary's reign on that part of the citadel outside the wall, but
by the end of 1557 it was still far from complete.

Adequate defences were as necessary then as ever. Mary lost Calais,
undermanned and inadequately maintained, on 7 January 1558. The
French king had been urging the Scots to attack England; and at
England's other outpost, Berwick, all the works which had been and
were being carried out were local improvements which only prolonged
the life of an obsolete system of defence.

The Elizabethan ramparts

In January 1558 an eminent English military engineer, Sir Richard Lee,
was ordered by the Queen to Berwick. Assisted by Ridgeway, he
replaced the landward medieval walls and castle by a modern bastioned

system. It was planned and begun under Mary. Most of the work was done in the next reign, and Lee's fortifications are known as the Elizabethan ramparts.

Berwick's defences were to be equal to the latest and best models of the age. Lee was especially qualified among his countrymen to undertake the task. He had designed the first English bastioned town fortification for Portsmouth in 1545, and since then had kept himself very well informed of continental developments.

We know from original plans that the design of the new fortification was changed several times before the actual building, but from the beginning, the northern part of the town and the castle were to be excluded and abandoned. The northern fronts were begun first. They had a central bastion (Cumberland Bastion) supported by two bastions which were at first only partly built (Meg's Mount and Brass Bastion); the latter were to be completed as symmetrical works similar to Cumberland Bastion.

The fortifications were carried out with compromises and alterations and were left incomplete. Reconstruction drawings of the designs for the fortifications intended late in 1558 (based on plans, documents and excavation) are given on pages 14–16.

In the original scheme all the bastions were to be similar, though because of modifications while building Brass now differs considerably from the others. The masonry walls of the bastions are 20ft high. They have long orillons to protect small two-storeyed flanking emplacements. Around the bastions, and behind the flankers, runs a cobbled sentry-path with a low breastwork. Above the sentry-path the rampart earthwork rises for a further 16ft to a cannon-proof parapet. The masonry would be protected from direct artillery fire by the outer wall or counterscarp of the ditch: fire could be directed only at the upper earthwork.

The illustrations on pages 14 and 15 show what was intended. The upper earthworks and the counterscarp were never begun as planned, the ditch left incomplete, the flankers altered—and at Brass the whole shape of the work was changed.

The masonry of the north fronts had been carried to a height of up to 14ft by 1560. Attention could be given to the fortification on the east side. By 1560 the area to be taken in was in dispute. The original intention had been to build a new curtain from the north-east angle running exactly on the line of the medieval wall and continuing in a

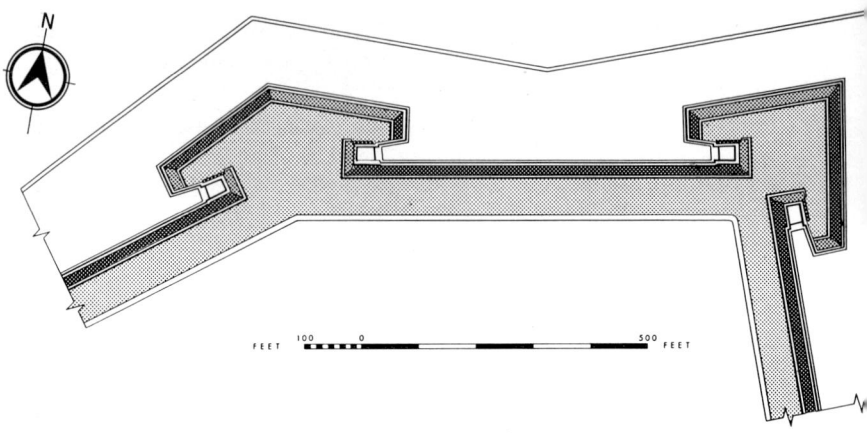

straight line to meet the partly-built Edward VI citadel, which was to
be completed and used as part of the new system. This involved the
preliminary demolition of the medieval wall and a serious weakening
of the town defences during the whole period of building. The construction of Brass Bastion had so far been curtailed to avoid such a
breach. An Italian engineer, Giovanni Portinari, was called in to advise
in 1560. Portinari made an opposite objection. He thought that Berwick
would be better protected by a line continuing the new north fronts
to the sea, cutting off the whole of the peninsula and thus preventing
infiltration along Magdalen Fields and the possibility of an attack on
both fronts.

Portinari's advice was heard and ignored. Instead the line of the east
fronts was revised to run completely within the medieval wall, with
the exception of the east face of Brass Bastion. The second stage of
construction, like the first, took in two lengths of curtain, with the
central bastion (Windmill) occupying a salient in the medieval wall;
a partly-built bastion by the river estuary to the south (King's Mount);
and another small portion of Brass. Until Brass was completed, the
old defences would still be unbroken. The design of the works closely
followed the pattern established in the north, and the speed of building
was kept up; at the beginning of the 1561 season over 1000 men were
employed. By October 1561 the east fronts had been raised to a maxi-
mum height of 14ft. This part of the design included the surviving gate,
Cowport.

A reconstruction drawing of Brass Bastion as proposed in 1558.
Top: half-plan from above showing earthworks.
Bottom: half-plan at ground level showing masonry structures.
Note the original small two-storeyed flankers

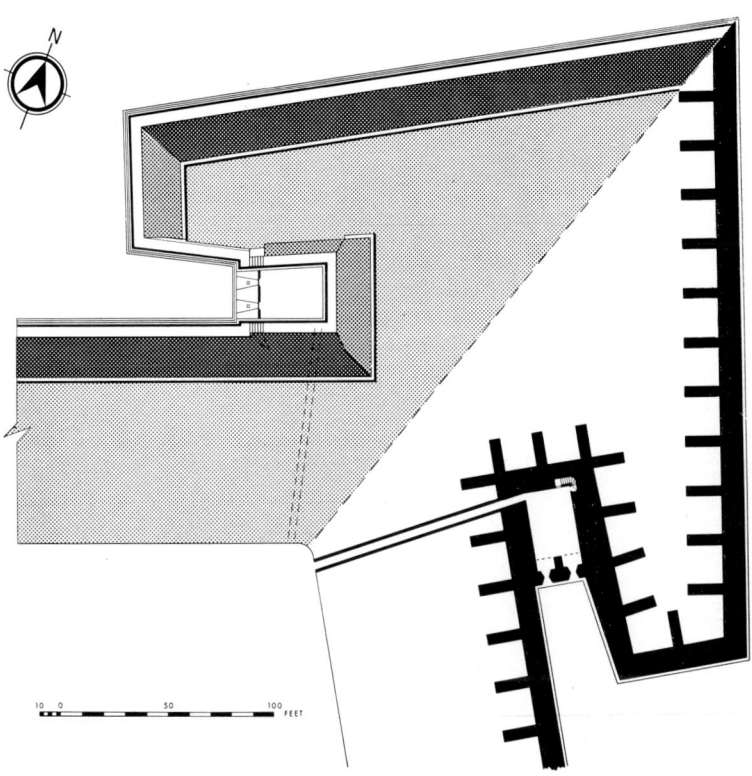

A start had also been made on the south fronts towards the river. These, too, had been a subject of controversy. The lower town contained the royal storehouses near the harbour and it could not lightly be abandoned, though Berwick would have been more secure if it were completely excluded from the fortifications. At first, while King's Mount was being built, it was intended to take in at least part of the lower town. But very soon afterwards the plan was changed. Work on the south fronts in 1561–62 was on a line which kept to the high ground between Meg's Mount and King's Mount.

There is now no trace of any fortification on the line between the salient angles of Meg's and King's. It is possible that the foundations only were laid, for the working force was reduced in 1562, and in 1563 crisis in France stopped work at Berwick altogether.

*A reconstruction drawing in perspective of Brass Bastion as
proposed in 1558: compare the plan given on page 15
Contrast the present state of the bastion with this symmetrical
design, with two-storeyed flankers, continuous sentry-path
and earthwork rampart rising above it*

Lee returned to Berwick in April 1564 and set about the completion
of Brass Bastion. The change of the line in the east had greatly distorted
the plan, originally meant to be symmetrical, and Lee had to make
alterations in order to allow more space on top of the bastion. By this
time, the two-storeyed design for the flankers had been abandoned.

While the layout of Brass was being completed, an adjacent length
of the medieval wall fractured and had to be demolished. This event
caused anxiety in London. Giovanni Portinari was again called in, with
another Italian and an English engineer. They had instructions to
confer on the whole subject of the Berwick fortifications.

The consultants differed among themselves, but agreed that the
fortifications should have taken in the whole width of the peninsula and
the flankers were much too small and inaccessible. Portinari quoted an
incident during the siege of Ambleteuse in 1549 (defended by the
English against the French) when a similar flanker was put out of action
by a single hit. Compromises were agreed on both points. An auxiliary
line, called a traverse, was taken from a point just south of Brass

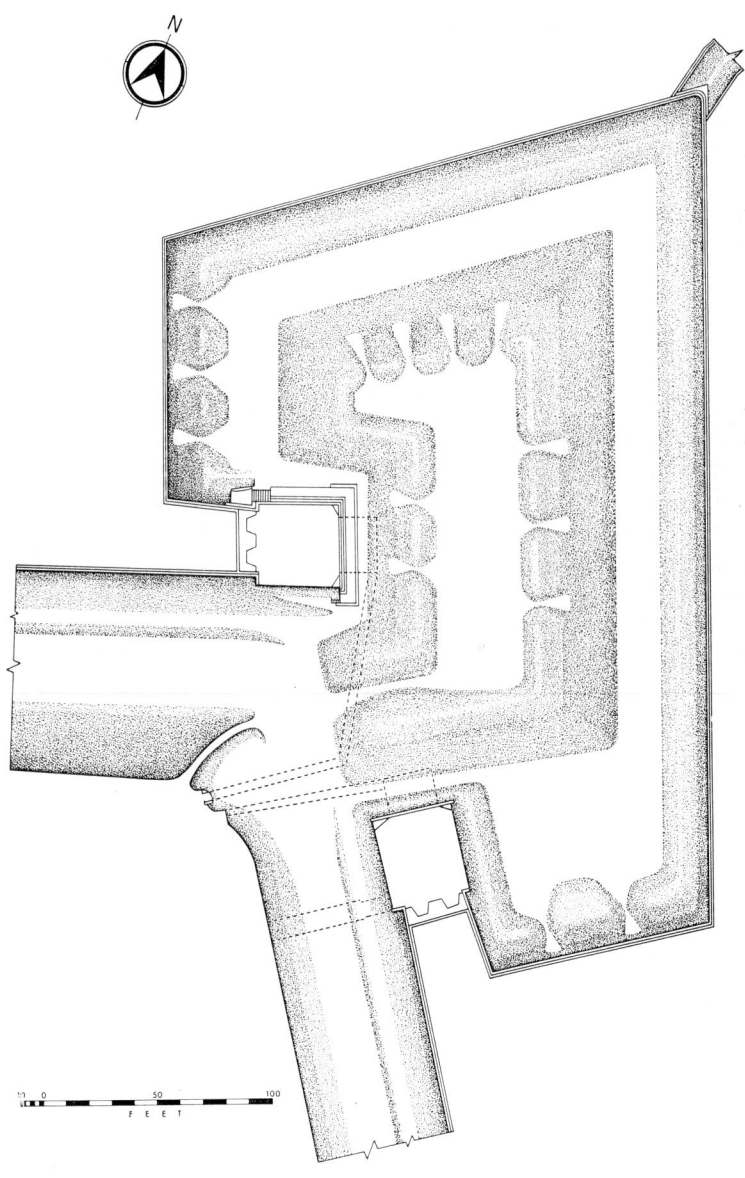

Brass Bastion: plan of present state. The arched-over rear parts of the enlarged flankers, and their access tunnels, are shown in broken line. The seventeenth-century earthwork parapets and cavalier are shown by a stipple. A length of the Elizabethan sentry-path is preserved over the rear of the west flanker

FEET

Bastion to the sea. Thus the peninsula was cut off. The flankers were enlarged and a start was made to improve the flanker access.

On several other points of criticism nothing was done, partly through Lee's obstinacy, partly because the Elizabethan works soon ended with the fortifications incomplete. Masonwork continued into 1566, but almost all the workmen were soon discharged. Though operations were resumed on the ditch, nothing seems to have been done after 1569.

In 1569 the upper earthworks of the rampart had not even been started. The ditch was never completed, the counterscarp wall never begun. Lee's system, without its intended earthworks on top of and outside the ramparts, was critically weakened. And the fortification between King's Bastion and Meg's Mount begun in 1561–62 was abandoned. The medieval wall continued as the only defence towards the river.

From the beginning of 1558 until the autumn of 1570 the total expenditure on works at Berwick was £128 648 5s 9½d, an average of about £9900 each year. The Berwick fortifications were the costliest undertaking of Elizabeth's reign.

Though their military value remained dubious to the end, the mere undertaking of the Elizabethan fortifications probably served a useful political purpose as a display of resolution. While they were under construction, the threat from Scotland increased with substantial French intervention to support the Regent, Mary of Lorraine; while the 1560 Treaty of Edinburgh relaxed the military situation, Elizabeth was insecure as long as Mary Queen of Scots endeavoured to assert her authority. (In the eyes of the Catholic sovereigns of Europe, Mary had a better claim to the English throne than Elizabeth.) Mary's final defeat at Langside, her imprisonment, her flight to England in 1568 and the consequent suspension of the Franco-Scottish alliance reduced the danger, and the works at Berwick came to an end. Near the end of the century the unacknowledged probability that James VI of Scotland would unite the crowns of the two countries led to a progressive improvement in relations. In the later years of Elizabeth and during the whole of James's reign as monarch of Great Britain, Berwick was neglected. The only considerable work was the protracted construction of a fine stone bridge across the Tweed, begun in 1611.

The crowns of England and Scotland were united, but the aspirations and interests of the two countries were not. Charles I's attempt to impose uniformity of church discipline led to rebellion in Scotland in 1638. Berwick was occupied by the Earl of Essex on 2 April 1639; Charles arrived in the town in May, and articles of pacification were signed there with the Scots on 7 June. The pacification brought about an uneasy armed truce, which gave an opportunity to strengthen Berwick's defences.

When the English Civil War began Berwick successfully resisted the Earl of Newcastle's attack in 1643; it was subsequently occupied by the Scots until 1645 when the Scottish army in England was disbanded. In the earlier years of Cromwell's Protectorate, Berwick remained a garrisoned frontier town of high importance. Improvements to the fortifications continued until 1653.

In 1639–53 an earthwork parapet was raised on the sentry-path right round the Elizabethan ramparts, and cavaliers (high earthwork platforms to mount guns firing out into the field) were raised on all the bastions. At this time the earthworks of the bastions and curtains were given the form which substantially exists today, though they were repaired and modified in detail in the middle of the eighteenth century.

Even so, the works were still much weaker than Lee had intended. And by the later seventeenth century they were obsolescent. This was the age of Marshal Vauban, Louis XIV's engineer, whose refined and complex fortifications set new high standards of defensive strength.

Surveys of Berwick were ordered, but the lessened strategic importance of the town did not justify the cost of substantial improvements. Between 1653 and 1747, only minor works and repairs were carried out on the fortifications.

Ravensdowne Barracks

Within the town, proper accommodation was at last provided for the garrison. The soldiers had been billeted in inns and sometimes in private houses. The practice was bad both for public relations and for discipline. Berwick Corporation began to urge the building of barracks in 1705, and the repercussions of the 1715 rebellion finally decided the building of Ravensdowne Barracks. In 1717 the Board of Ordnance approved the spending of £4937 10s 7d on barracks for 36 officers and 600 men. Work was begun on two barrack blocks facing each other across a large square. The buildings were occupied in 1721. The entrance is by a central gatehouse in a screen wall. The design has been attributed to

Sir John Vanbrugh, and there is a clear sympathy between the architectural part of military engineering and the genius of England's great Baroque architect. But the designer of Ravensdowne is an unknown engineer officer.

In the early eighteenth century there was no tradition of barrack planning. The first buildings at Ravensdowne provided little more than living and sleeping accommodation for the garrison. Apart from the barrack blocks, there was only the guard-house at the gate and a small store opposite it. The plan was too simple. In 1730 a nearby private house was acquired for a hospital, and in 1739–41 the south range (the Clock Block) was built as a storehouse. In the eighteenth century there was no mess and no cookhouse: the officers had their meals brought to them in their apartments; the men prepared their food in the small barrack rooms.

Ravensdowne became the depot of the King's Own Borderers (later the King's Own Scottish Borderers) in 1881; although the regiment finally marched out in 1964, the barracks retain the regimental headquarters and museum.

The defences after 1746

The last attempt to improve the security of Berwick was inspired by the alarm caused by the Jacobite rising of 1745–46. The works were not greatly altered: the Elizabethan landward fronts with their seventeenth-century earthworks, and the medieval riverside walls, all now useless as serious fortifications, were carefully repaired. Large breaches in the scarp walls were made good, some changes were made to the line of the riverside defences, the earthworks were re-formed and perhaps strengthened. The present state of the fortifications is almost exactly as it was in the third quarter of the eighteenth century. One particular improvement was the provision of a bomb-proof magazine, built in 1749.

During the Napoleonic wars it was proposed to abandon those works which could not be used for the defence of the estuary. The end of Berwick as a fortified town is marked by the enlargement of Scotsgate and the insertion of Ness Gate leading to the new pier in 1815–16. In 1825 the Bridge Gate was removed, and in 1837 the pedestrian way along the ramparts was made. In 1852 and 1864 the greater part of the Elizabethan ramparts was leased by the Crown to the local authority, and in 1877 the latter purchased the Elizabethan north fronts for £100.

By the terms of the leases, the town carried out limited repairs to the ramparts.

Active interest in the fortifications as an antiquity began with a protest over the proposed demolition of part of the north medieval wall near the Bell Tower in 1903–04. As a result, the Office of Works took the remains of this part of the wall into its guardianship as an ancient monument; and the Berwick Historic Monuments Committee was set up by local initiative to promote conservation elsewhere. A tangible result of the Committee's activities was the clearance of some of the flankers.

Limited preservation was carried out by the Office of Works on the length of the riverside walls remaining in Crown ownership. Preservation was resumed on a comprehensive scale after 1931, when the north fronts were given into guardianship by Berwick Town Council.

A Tour of
the Fortifications

The fortifications and other works will be described as they are seen while walking round them. The description begins from Scotsgate with the Elizabethan ramparts at Meg's Mount, and continues round Cumberland Bastion, Brass Bastion, Cowport—with a diversion to take in Ravensdowne Barracks (page 29)—and Windmill Bastion to the Tweed estuary at King's Mount. The medieval walls are then followed (pages 32–33) along the Tweed by the seventeenth-century bridge to the castle (pages 33–34) and from the castle by the Bell Tower and Lord's Mount for the remainder of the circuit of the medieval walls. This route may be followed on the general plan at the end of the text. It may be broken up into convenient lengths. For a short visit the length from Scotsgate to Brass Bastion gives a good picture of the Elizabethan ramparts.

Scotsgate

Scotsgate opens through the Elizabethan curtain between Meg's Mount and Cumberland Bastion. It guarded the main road to Scotland: traffic on the Great North Road still passes through it. The entry originally resembled Cowport, but was rebuilt and widened in 1815 and further altered in 1858. There is an access path on each side of Scotsgate leading up to the ramparts.

Meg's Mount

The Elizabethan works were started in 1558 at Meg's Mount and were continued eastward. Meg's was intended to be a complete bastion, but only the eastern half was built: the defences are continued along the river by the reconstructed medieval wall. The details of Meg's are similar to those described below at Cumberland Bastion.

The two paths round the ramparts were laid out in 1837. The lower path is at the level of the terreplein or fighting platform as established in the seventeenth century. The upper path runs along the top of the thick earthen parapet. As built, the back of the parapet was much steeper, with a firing-step. Between Meg's and Cumberland, the area of the ditch in front of the ramparts was raised and surfaced as the cattle market in 1886. It is now used as a car park. Because of the raising of the level, the visible walls of the rampart are misleadingly low. Their true height is first clearly seen beyond Cumberland Bastion.

Cumberland Bastion

Cumberland Bastion is a complete and regular work. The masonry is Elizabethan; all the earthworks above the masonry were raised in 1639–53. Approaching Cumberland from Scotsgate, the west flanking emplacement or flanker can be seen protected by the long narrow flat-headed orillon of the bastion. The west flanker (partly refaced following the Elizabethan design in work begun in 1971) is similar to the better-preserved east flanker, which will be described in detail.

The earthworks on the bastion are a parapet right round the masonry scarp and a high central platform, called a cavalier, with its own parapet. Guns were mounted on both levels, and some of the embrasures may still be seen. The size and shape of the bastion and its relation to the whole system may be appreciated from the cavalier. The guns mounted in the flankers could scour the whole front as far as the salient angle of the next bastion. The cross-fire of guns mounted in opposed flanks is the basic defensive idea of the bastioned system.

The planning of the flankers and the alterations made to them are seen in the east flanker of Cumberland.* A narrow rear part of the flanker widens by splayed side walls to the front. The rear part survives from the small flankers built in 1558–59. In the south wall, a doorway with a four-centered head gives access to a 3ft wide tunnel leading through the rampart earthwork to the town. In the north wall a similar opening leads by a stair in the thickness of the wall to a doorway at a higher level. A heavy timber deck was originally laid across the flanker at the sill level of the upper doorway. The deck carried a second tier of flanking guns. The joist-holes for some of the timbers supporting the deck may be seen in a narrow course of masonry at the rear of the flanker. Beside each of the lower doorways are small square recesses, probably magazines for ready-use ammunition. In the rear wall is a larger arched recess of unknown function: similar recesses on the side walls were obliterated in the enlargement described below.

The small size of the flankers was criticised, and after 1564 they were enlarged to their present form. The original cross-walls of the flankers were demolished and most of their side walls partly cut away. The enlargement was first tried experimentally at Brass Bastion, where the

---

*On request the custodian, normally on duty on the ramparts or at Ravensdowne Barracks, will open the east flanker of Cumberland Bastion and the west flanker of Brass to visitors. All the other flankers have to be kept shut for security.

rear parts of the flankers had already been arched over to widen the gorge of the bastion (one of the arches may be seen from Cumberland). In the Brass enlargement the rear parts were left alone. Soon the flankers of the other bastions were enlarged and the pattern established at Brass was followed, though the rear arches did not exist in the other bastions.

The cut-away side walls were then re-faced and jointed to the narrow rear part by splays. New cross-walls were built nearer the orillon head. Immediately behind the frontal walls are brick-arched recesses intended as entries to never-built access tunnels. The upper parts of the frontal walls were reconstructed in 1690 and 1715. Their Elizabethan form is preserved on the face only up to the sill level of unsplayed gun ports. A break in the masonry of the Elizabethan sills was caused by blocking the ports in 1719.

In this flanker as elsewhere, a considerable amount of the ashlar facework has been renewed, most conspicuously in the large-scale repairs after 1747. The ditch in front of the curtain between Cumberland and Brass remains in much the same state as when it was left incomplete in the reign of Elizabeth, except that a secondary narrow ditch dug in the middle of the main ditch in 1565 has now been filled up. The outer side or counterscarp of the main ditch was to be finished by a masonry wall equal in height to the bold half-round moulding, the cordon, which encircles the ramparts.

Brass Bastion

A reconstruction of the original design for Brass (showing the detail for all the other bastions) is given as a perspective drawing on page 16. The present view of Brass approached from Cumberland Bastion may be compared with this drawing. The present state of Brass in plan is given on page 17. At Brass Bastion, a cobbled path is exposed above the rear arch and along part of one side of the west flanker. This is the only part now visible of the Elizabethan sentry-path which ran around the whole circuit of the ramparts. A short length of the low coped breastwork of the sentry-path survives. The sentry-path could also be used as a line of defence for foot-soldiers. It was intended that artillery should be mounted at a higher level, on an upper earthwork rising above and behind the sentry-path. The upper earthwork, proposed for

Aerial view of Brass Bastion (above) and Cumberland Bastion (below)

all the bastions and curtains, was never begun. It would have resembled the existing seventeenth-century cavaliers, though wider and higher.

Brass Bastion has a more complicated building history than any of the other bastions, and the complications affect the design. The plan of the bastion was distorted by the change of alignment of the Elizabethan east fronts (page 16). As a result of the distortion, the gorge of the bastion was awkwardly narrowed. In 1564 Sir Richard Lee arched over the rear parts of the flankers to carry the sentry-path and so widen the gorge. Hence the deep arches at Brass which appear nowhere else. By this date the idea of upper gun decks in the flankers (discussed at Cumberland, page 25) had been abandoned and the doors and stair at the flanker rear were never built.

The Brass flankers were the first to be enlarged as described at Cumberland. Behind the frontal wall is a broad access tunnel intended to be cut through the rampart to the town. It was left unfinished in the west flanker. Opposite it is a smaller arch cut as an approach to an intended sallyport in the return wall of the orillon.

An incomplete postern in the curtain between Brass and Cumberland is visible from the west orillon head of Brass Bastion.

From the salient angle of Brass, a low grass-covered wall extends across the ditch. This was built as a dam to retain water in the ditch at different levels at each side of it. When standing on the salient angle one can see the line of the medieval wall with its ditch running northward to the circular gun tower called Lord's Mount, built by Henry VIII (beside the house with the red roof). West of Lord's Mount the upper stages of the Bell Tower are visible above modern rooftops.

The east flanker of Brass is similar to the west. The beam-holes in the rear parts of both the Brass flankers are an eighteenth-century insertion, when the arches were walled up and intermediate floors inserted for use as temporary magazines.

Brass Bastion stands on the north-east angle of the bastioned circuit. East of the ramparts lie Magdalen Fields, used as a golf course. This has been an open space during the whole history of Berwick. The building of the ramparts was accompanied by controversy on whether or not the fields should be taken within the fortification. The compromise eventually reached in 1564 was to lead a traverse line from a point just south of Brass Bastion to the sea, where it ended in an earthwork redoubt. The ditch of the traverse, and the remains of the redoubt, may be seen from the seaward face of Brass.

Cowport

Cowport is the only surviving gateway in the Elizabethan ramparts. Scotsgate was similar. Cowport is a vaulted tunnel through the rampart, slightly angled where it was defended by a portcullis. The wooden gate was made about 1750. The outer face of Cowport has a row of corbels presumably surviving from an upper structure enclosing the portcullis mechanism and perhaps displaying the arms of Elizabeth. The cordon which now confusingly runs above the corbels was built after 1747.

Ravensdowne Barracks

From Cowport an access leads down from the rampart to Ravensdowne Barracks, designed in 1717. The elevation facing the Parade joins the gables of the two main blocks by a screen wall. The gables and the central gateway in the screen wall are finished with a military baroque severity. The gateway is splendidly decorated with the arms of George I. The arms are quartered: 1 England and Scotland; 2 France; 3 Ireland; 4 Hanover (with its white horse and the golden crown of Charlemagne). The French arms were kept on the British royal arms until the title of King of France was discontinued in 1801. The arms of Hanover, introduced by George I as Elector of Hanover, were kept until Victoria became Queen of Great Britain in 1837, when the Hanoverian throne passed to the nearest male heir. Until 1806 the ruler of Hanover was one of the German princes who formally elected the Holy Roman Emperor: hence the golden crown on the arms.

In the barrack square, the general appearance of the masses of building has been little changed since the eighteenth century. There are two original three-storeyed main blocks, each with three staircases of barrack accommodation and a terminal north pavilion for officers. Opposite the main gate is a separate two-storeyed block which was built in 1739–41 as a storehouse and later enlarged to hold the barrack offices. The barracks were designed to accommodate 36 officers and 600 men. The accommodation scale allowed eight men to each barrack room in four double beds. At first the barracks provided accommodation and little else. There were no welfare services; and there was also no hospital and no cookhouse—the men prepared their meals in the barrack-rooms. Ravensdowne was continuously adapted to changing needs and was garrisoned by regular troops until 1964. The King's Own Scottish Borderers, associated with Ravensdowne since 1881, have their regimental museum in the east block.

Medieval Wall

Just south of Cowport the rampart walk slopes down. This represents a change of level in the ditch and the site of an intended dam similar to that existing at Brass. From this point on to King's Mount, the medieval defences are visible as a broad earthen mound outside the Elizabethan ramparts. The surviving masonry of the medieval wall and its towers lie beneath the earthen covering. Part of the earthwork was raised by Edward I, whose palisaded bank and ditch was the earliest substantial fortification of Berwick town. Later a stone wall replaced the timber palisade. The earthwork was augmented in the first half of the sixteenth century, when the medieval wall seems to have been lowered and strengthened to improve its resistance to artillery bombardment.

Windmill Bastion: Edward VI Citadel

Windmill Bastion is similar to Cumberland, though it is slightly larger. Both the lower platform and the cavalier of Windmill have gun mountings dating from the nineteenth century to the First World War. The guns were used for the defence of the approaches to the river.

Massive earthworks beyond the medieval wall may be seen from Windmill. The most northerly is Windmill Bulwark, a large detached earthwork surrounded by its own ditch, raised by Richard Cavendish in 1522-23.

The southerly earthworks survive from the second stage of work on the Edward VI citadel, executed in 1557 by William Ridgeway, surveyor of Berwick, but never completed. The rest of the citadel was abandoned when the Elizabethan east fronts were built. The masonry scarps for this east part of the citadel may never have been begun, though the ditch was dug outside it. The plan of the citadel is given on page 10 and is related to the visible earthwork on the folding plan inside the back cover.

The counterscarp of the ditch which encloses all these earthworks has a small ledge cut into it. This is a covered way hastily and irregularly constructed in 1639-40. A covered way is a line of defence beyond the ditch protected or "covered" from hostile fire by a parapet. The stone revetment of its parapet may be seen in places from Windmill Bastion. It is not a typical example of such works, which are normally much broader.

A short distance south of Windmill, inside the rampart, stands the vaulted and buttressed magazine (at present used as a store) built in 1749 to replace the damp makeshift magazines in the flankers of Brass Bastion. It lies in the Edward VI citadel site.

Outside the Elizabethan ramparts, the citadel earthworks continue almost as far as King's Mount. They may be more closely viewed by passing through the Elizabethan ramparts by a modern tunnel (1895) a short distance north of King's Mount.

King's Mount

As with Meg's Mount, only half of King's Mount was built. The reasons for the controversy (page 15) over the best route for the rampart from King's are very clear on the ground. West from King's Mount the ground slopes steeply to the lower town. The slope is the best position for a defensive line. Below the slope, the town, whether encircled by ramparts or not, would be open to artillery fire from beyond the Tweed. In spite of the extent and value of the lower town, it was decided to exclude it and works were begun on a line at right angles from King's. Work on the line was abandoned at an early stage of building and no structures along it are now visible. The cavalier raised on King's Mount in 1639–53 was subsequently removed.

Riverside medieval walls

The salient angle of King's joins the medieval walls which continued in use as the defence of the town along the river. In the length of medieval wall beyond King's Mount is a half-round tower, the so-called Black Watchtower. The wall then descends to the shore and is pierced by Ness Gate, a modern passage (1816) leading to the pier. The medieval wall continues to a projecting battery called Fisher's Fort, partly rebuilt in the eighteenth century. It was originally constructed as "the Bulwark on the Sands" by Richard Cavendish in 1522–23. In its outer face, and visible from the beach, is a blocked water-gate. The battery still mounts a souvenir of the Crimean War.

The next two lengths of curtain were entirely rebuilt as far as Coxon Tower, and eighteenth-century works continue along the rest of the riverside walls up to Meg's Mount.

Coxon Tower

Coxon Tower is a quarter-round tower with a rib-vaulted lower chamber. There are two small apertures from the chamber through the thickness of the wall. Beyond the tower is a long battery mostly rebuilt and realigned in the eighteenth century. At the west end of the line of embrasures, a road leads down to Palace Green. Beside the road is the eighteenth-century guardhouse which stood near Scotsgate until 1815, when it was dismantled and re-erected here.

Quay walls

From Palace Green by the Shore Gate to the seventeenth-century bridge, the quay walls have houses built against their rear face. The houses include a fine custom house of about 1800. The Shore Gate, near the custom house, led to the quay. It was completely rebuilt in the eighteenth century as a segmental arch with rusticated masonry. Several passages lead through the walls to the quay from the cellars and yards of the houses immediately behind: a convenience to the inhabitants, but an appreciable security problem. There is also a sallyport close to the bridge.

Bridge

The fifteen-arched bridge was begun in 1611 to replace the medieval wooden bridge which was further upstream. The seventeenth-century bridge rises slowly from the south to the highest arch, the fourteenth, negotiable for small vessels. The refuges above the higher piers in the northern part of the bridge, which was built first, are ornamented with small attached columns. The bridge carried the Great North Road until 1928, when the Royal Tweed Bridge was opened.

Riverside wall

The riverside wall, still on the medieval line though its visible masonry was almost entirely replaced in the eighteenth century, continues under and beyond the Royal Tweed Bridge. Near a boathouse, it climbs to the top of the escarpment in three massive steps. At the higher level, it continues north-west to be joined by Meg's Mount. A path leads round the face of the stepped wall and Meg's to reach Scotsgate. This completes the Elizabethan circuit.

From the boathouse the remains of the castle may best be seen by keeping to the riverside walk. The building of the Elizabethan ramparts cut off both the castle and the north part of the medieval walled town. A fragment of the medieval wall is visible on the bank beyond Meg's. The wall then turned to skirt the declivity known as Castle Dene.

Castle

The castle rose on the bluff on the opposite side of the dene. Although the castle was isolated by the construction of the Elizabethan works, it was not immediately abandoned: new lodgings, for example, were formed in it in 1600–03. The castle was used as a stone quarry in the eighteenth century, and in 1847 Stephenson's admirable Royal Border

Bridge brought the railway to run destructively through the middle of it.

The first part of the castle defences visible from the riverside walk is the White Wall, a spectacular blocking wall taken down the bluff from the castle to the river. The parapet wall is stepped and loop-holed; the walk is called Breakneck Stairs.

The wall is taken out to the river. Just by the river bank is a sixteenth-century gun tower. The riverside walk goes through the lower storey of the gun tower by a vaulted pend. The pend is defended by an angled loophole near the entry. Flanking it are three gun casemates with widely splayed ports. The casemates are narrow and low, and even though they were only meant for small pieces, they must have been very difficult to work. Increasing freedom of movement for the defender is one of the characteristics of the development of artillery fortification.

The first floor of the gun-tower has three emplacements for small swivel guns. Each emplacement (like the lower casemates) has a smoke-vent piercing the arch. The first floor also has a fireplace. The tower was probably finished by an open embrasured parapet.

The west wall of the castle survives because it formed the boundary for the railway yard. It is now in the guardianship of the Department. Attached to the wall, on top of the escarpment, is a second gun-tower, similar to the lower one in general design but not in detail. The surviving lower casemated level has been vaulted. It has three embrasures internally splayed and with four-centred heads. The bar-holes in the embrasures held a wooden beam into which the swivel of the gun was fixed. The storey above the lower casemate had a latrine. Except for the tower, the badly robbed wall has no clear features.

These are the only parts of the castle which are accessible: the polygonal fourteenth-century south-east tower survives but lies in private grounds.

North medieval walls

The path from the north-west walls of the castle leads out to the North Road. Turn south-west over the railway bridge and along Northumberland Avenue; this brings you to the remaining part of the north medieval walls. As on the east fronts, the ditch and earthen bank survive from the 1296 fortification of Berwick by Edward I. But his wooden palisade has been replaced by a 9ft-thick wall which survives in fragments.

Bell Tower

The Bell Tower stands conspicuously in the middle of the earthen mound of the rampart. The tower is octagonal with four storeys. All of its upper part is a late Tudor rebuild. Though the wall has been removed on each side down to its lowest courses, the doors giving access to the parapet walk show its original height.

Lord's Mount

The north-east angle of the medieval town wall lies a little way further east. This vulnerable part of the defences was strengthened in 1522–23 by an earthen bulwark, now very indistinct. In 1539–42 the earthwork was succeeded by a circular masonry fortification, now called Lord's Mount (page 9), excavated in 1972–73. The surviving parts of its massive outer wall have six artillery casements, one of them blocked, fireplaces and a latrine. The fortification now rises only to the height of the timber deck which covered the lower casemated floor. An upper floor level and the parapet level have been demolished. The lower casemates were vaulted and have small expense magazines (originally fitted with doors) in their sides. They were first armed with long swivel guns (holes for the swivel pins are cut in the gunport sills), soon replaced by carriage-mounted pieces for which the casemate floors were raised. In the centre of the fortification is a light-well with openings cut in it to give borrowed light, as well as ventilation, to the ground floor.

The kitchen for the garrison occupied the east part of the work. Its
12ft wide fireplace with an oven, and its well with a chase for the
wheel of the winding mechanism cut in the adjacent wall-face, may
still be seen.

In 1545 further earthworks, in the shape of an angular bastion, were
proposed beyond Lord's Mount by an Italian engineer.

When the Elizabethan ramparts were built Lord's Mount became
redundant, and as it was high enough to overlook the Elizabethan
north front its upper part was demolished. The interior was levelled
off and a parapet added in 1639–53, when it was pressed into emergency
service as a high-level battery.

Spades Mire

A little way to the north of Lord's Mount is the ditch known as Spades Mire. Its date and function are unknown. It seems to be part of an outer line of defence first constructed during one of the military crises of Berwick's medieval history. Spades Mire is not in the guardianship of the Department of the Environment.

Brass Bastion–Cumberland Bastion

From Lord's Mount a path leads outside the medieval ditch to the salient of Brass Bastion. The tour is completed by walking along the outer face of the north Elizabethan fronts back to Scotsgate.

The dam at the salient of Brass was meant to be finished by a stone cope. The stub of the cope is built out from the facework of the bastion. A channel to control the sluice is cut on the south face of the dam. The cordon and plinth of the bastion change level to correspond to the change of level of the bottom of the ditch on each side of the dam.

In the curtain between Brass and Cumberland is an incomplete postern, from which a stone causeway and wooden bridge were intended to lead out across the ditch. From Brass Bastion to Meg's Mount the great and costly Elizabethan works present themselves in an imposing line: Lord Hunsdon, appointed governor of Berwick in November 1568, justly described the new walls as "marvellous beautiful." But from beyond the ditch it is clear how vulnerable they were without the protection of the high counterscarp wall. The ground level beyond the ditch is mostly below the level of the intended counterscarp and would have been made up if the counterscarp had ever been built. In 1568, in spite of its marvellous beautiful walls, the town was still "very bare and ungardable"–and so it continued for the rest of its military history.

FURTHER READING

The History of the King's Works, ed. H. M. Colvin and Dr A. J. Taylor, 1963, s.v. "Berwick."
Iain MacIvor, "The Elizabethan Fortifications of Berwick-upon-Tweed," in *The Antiquaries' Journal,* 1965, Vol. XLV, Part I, pp. 65–96.
John Scott, *Berwick-upon-Tweed,* 1888.

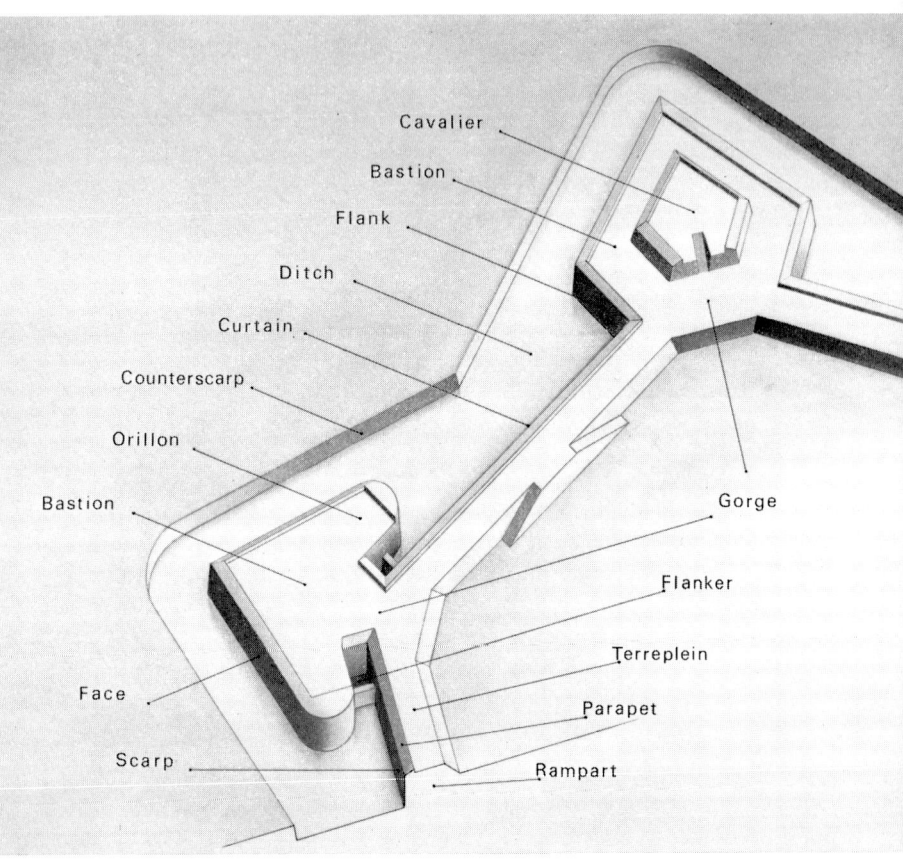

Cavalier

Bastion

Flank

Ditch

Curtain

Counterscarp

Orillon

Bastion

Gorge

Flanker

Terreplein

Face

Parapet

Scarp

Rampart

MILITARY engineers used a number of technical words to describe the elements of an artillery fortification. The list opposite gives a short definition of the technical words in this handbook. Some of the elements are illustrated in photographs and drawings throughout the book—and these are referred to in the definitions. Most of the elements are illustrated in the drawing above, and these are marked by asterisks. The drawing is only a block diagram of a simple fortification. It is not copied from any individual work.

Glossary

BASTIONS*   The strongpoints of an artillery fortification, corresponding to the towers of a medieval castle or town wall. All bastions have two *faces meeting at an angle. In some forms (on left of diagram opposite), as at Berwick, the faces end in *orillons or "ears." The orillons may be either rounded, as in diagram or squared, as at Berwick. The orillons protect flanking gun emplacements or *flankers. Other forms of bastion (top right of diagram) omit the flankers and have simpler straight *flanks directly joining the faces to the *curtains.

CASEMATE   A vaulted or roofed gun emplacement.

CAVALIER*   A gun platform raised above the level of a bastion or curtain to improve the field of fire.

CORDON   A bold half-round moulding at the top of the *scarp dividing the scarp from the *parapet.

COUNTERFORT   An internal buttress of scarp and counterscarp walls (diagram on page 15).

COUNTERSCARP*   The wall-face or sloped earthwork face bounding the outside of the ditch.

CURTAIN*   The length of rampart between two bastions.

DITCH*   A wide flat-bottomed ditch in front of the rampart was scoured by fire from the bastion flanks.

FACE*   The straight sides of a bastion towards the field, meeting in a point, are called the faces. They give all varieties of the bastion plan a characteristic angular shape.

FLANK*   The faces of a bastion are joined to the curtains by the flanks.

FLANKER*   A gun emplacement recessed into the flank of a bastion.

GORGE*   The "throat" the narrowest part of a bastion at the junction of the flanks with the curtains.

ORILLON*   A rounded or square-ended elongation of a bastion, protecting a flanker.

PARAPET*   A wall of masonry, brick or earthwork, usually thick enough to resist cannon fire, raised on top of the rampart to protect the defenders.

RAMPART*   The massive and continuous work of bastions and curtains around a fortified place. The rampart may be completely of earth, or it may have a stone or brick *scarp backed with earth.

REDOUBT   A work detached from the main fortification but forming part of the complete system of defence.

SCARP*   The sloping front of the rampart, rising from the bottom of the ditch to the cordon at parapet level.

TERREPLEIN*   The broad level fighting-platform of bastions and curtains behind the parapets.

The list excludes all elements of bastioned fortification which in its later development became very complex and are not relevant to Berwick.

CONVERSION TABLE

1ft	0.3m	30yd	27.4m
5ft	1.5m	35yd	32.0m
10ft	3.0m	40yd	36.6m
15ft	4.6m	45yd	41.1m
20ft	6.1m	50yd	45.7m
25ft	7.6m	100yd	91.4m
30ft	9.1m	200yd	182.9m
35ft	10.7m	300yd	274.3m
40ft	12.2m	400yd	365.8m
45ft	13.7m	500yd	457.2m
50ft	15.2m	1000yd	914.4m
100ft	30.5m		
		1 acre	0.40 hectare
1yd	0.9m	5 acres	2.02 hectares
5yd	4.6m	10 acres	4.05 hectares
10yd	9.1m		
15yd	13.7m	1 mile	1.60km
20yd	18.3m	5 miles	8.04km
25yd	22.9m	10 miles	16.09km

Printed in Scotland by Her Majesty's Stationery Office at HMSO Press, Edinburgh
Dd 496973 K96 9/76 (13675)

THE FORTIFICATIONS OF BERWICK-UPON-TWEED

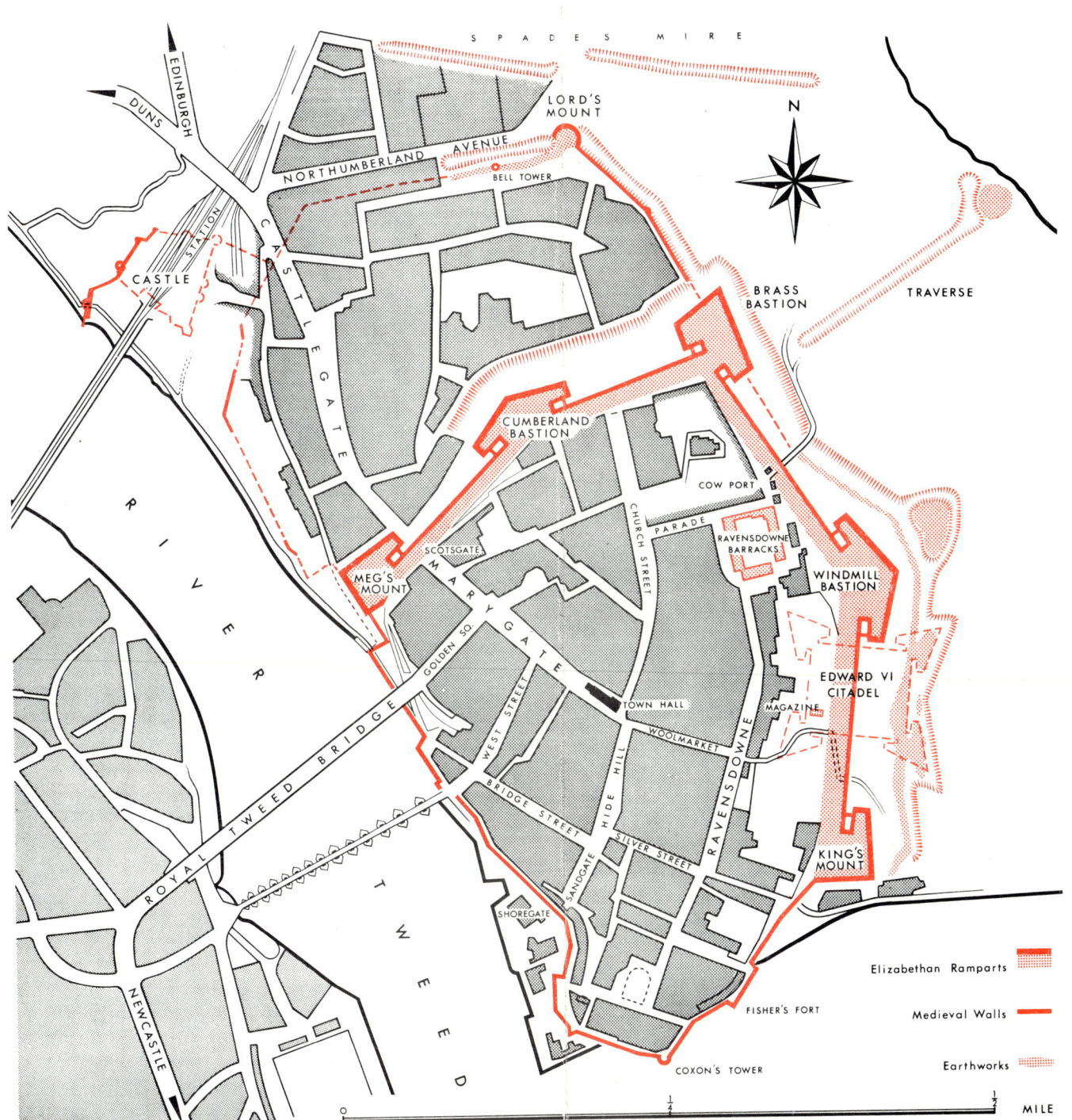

SPADES MIRE

EDINBURGH

DUNS

CASTLE STATION

NORTHUMBERLAND AVENUE

CASTLE

CASTLEGATE

LORD'S MOUNT

BELL TOWER

N

TRAVERSE

BRASS BASTION

CUMBERLAND BASTION

COW PORT

CHURCH STREET

PARADE

RAVENSDOWNE BARRACKS

WINDMILL BASTION

SCOTSGATE

MEG'S MOUNT

MARYGATE

GOLDEN SQ.

EDWARD VI CITADEL

R I V E R

WEST STREET

TOWN HALL

MAGAZINE

BRIDGE STREET

HIDE HILL

WOOLMARKET

SILVER STREET

RAVENSDOWNE

KING'S MOUNT

ROYAL TWEED BRIDGE

SANDGATE

SHOREGATE

FISHER'S FORT

NEWCASTLE

T W E E D

COXON'S TOWER

Elizabethan Ramparts

Medieval Walls

Earthworks

0   ¼   ½

MILE